I0841931

Raw Feelings

A Radical Dive into the Depths of Emotions Theory and Experience

Freudian Trips

Copyright

© 2023 by Freudian Trips

All rights reserved. No part of this book may be reproduced in any form or by any electronic or mechanical means, including information storage and retrieval systems, without permission in writing from the publisher, except by a reviewer who may quote brief passages in a review.

This book is a work of non-fiction. Unless otherwise noted, the author and the publisher make no explicit guarantees as to the accuracy of the information contained in this book and will not be held responsible for any errors or omissions.

Published by Omniterra Media Inc

First Edition

Visit the author's website at www.freudiantrips.com

Disclaimer

The views and opinions expressed in this book are those of the author(s) and do not necessarily reflect the official policy or position of any other agency, organization, employer, or company. The contents of this book are for informational and educational purposes only and are not intended to serve as professional advice, diagnosis, or treatment.

The information provided in this book is believed to be accurate and reliable as of the date of publication. However, it may include some errors or inaccuracies, and no warranty or guarantee is provided regarding the accuracy, timeliness, or applicability of the content.

Readers are encouraged to consult with professional philosophers, educators, or other qualified professionals where appropriate for personalized advice. The author(s) and publisher shall not be liable for any loss, damage, or harm caused or alleged to be caused, directly or indirectly, by the information or ideas contained, suggested, or referenced in this book.

By reading this book, the reader acknowledges and agrees that they are solely responsible for how they interpret and apply the information contained herein.

This book may also include references to other works, studies, and sources. These references are provided for further reading and exploration and do not imply endorsement or validation of the specific theories, viewpoints, or interpretations presented in those works.

Tuning Into the Symphony of Emotions: A Friendly Introduction

The Curtain Rises: A Peek into Emotion's Past

Imagine sitting in a grand theatre. The curtain rises, and the stage is set for one of the most intriguing performances you'll ever witness: the story of human emotion. This isn't just any story. It's a tale that stretches back to the dawn of humanity and even beyond, to the time when our distant ancestors first began to feel. Over the years, many great minds have tried to decipher this complex script, to understand what emotions really are and why we have them.

A long time ago, philosophers like Aristotle believed emotions were tied to the balance of bodily fluids. Fast forward a few centuries, and we find scholars like Charles Darwin proposing that emotions evolved as signals, helping humans communicate and bond with each other. As the spotlights moved through time, the theories multiplied, each trying to unravel the dance of emotions within us.

Let's Get Acquainted: Emotions, Feelings, and Moods

Now, before we go any deeper, let's clear up some common misunderstandings. You might think, "Aren't emotions, feelings, and moods all the same?" Well, not exactly. Imagine you're watching a beautiful sunset. The immediate reaction you have? That's emotion. It's raw and instant. Think of it as the actors' first appearance on our grand stage.

Now, as you process that emotion, thinking about how the sunset makes you nostalgic or how it reminds you of a cherished memory, that's a feeling. It's a more personal, internal response to the emotion you've experienced. If emotions are the actors, feelings are the monologues they deliver, rich with backstory and depth.

But wait, there's one more character we need to meet: moods. If you've been feeling cheerful all day without any specific reason, or perhaps a bit blue, that's your mood. Moods are like the backdrop on our stage. They set the tone but might not be directly linked to a specific event or stimulus.

Preparing for the Voyage: Our Emotion-Filled Expedition

As we journey through this book, we'll sail through the vast seas of emotions, diving deep to uncover hidden treasures and sailing through storms to find clarity. Here's a sneak peek of what's ahead:

Discovering Emotion's Blueprint: We'll delve into the very foundation of emotions, exploring how our brains and bodies play a role in making us feel.

The Colors of Emotion: We'll identify the different shades and nuances of emotions, from the bubbling joy of laughter to the searing pain of loss.

Mastering the Art of Emotion: Just like a captain learns to navigate the seas, we'll learn how to harness and guide our emotions for a more fulfilling life.

Connecting Heartbeats: Emotions aren't just individual experiences. They bridge the gap between hearts. We'll see how emotions play a role in our relationships, friendships, and even in the digital age.

So, take a deep breath. Feel the excitement? That's emotion. Reflect on how this chapter made you feel. That's a feeling. And if you're curious and eager for the chapters to come, well, that's the mood we hope to set for the rest of this book. Buckle up; it's going to be an exhilarating journey through the fascinating world of emotions!

Chapter 1: Inside the Control Room: The Science Behind Our Feelings

The Invisible Messengers: Understanding Neurotransmitters

Let's imagine for a moment that our brains are bustling cities. Streets are busy, skyscrapers reach for the clouds, and every day, countless messages are passed around. These vital messages, responsible for everything from making you jump in surprise to feeling butterflies when you're in love, are carried by special messengers we call neuro-transmitters.

Think of neurotransmitters like postmen, dashing around the brain, delivering letters of emotion. Sometimes these letters contain joyful news, making you feel elated. Other times, they might bring a sad note, causing a pang in your heart. These messengers play a massive part in determining how we feel at any given moment.

Three Remarkable Landmarks: Amygdala, Hippocampus, and Prefrontal Cortex

Within our brain's bustling city, there are a few essential landmarks that play a massive role in the world of emotions.

The Amygdala: Picture the amygdala as the city's alert system. Whenever there's something important - say a surprise party or a lurking danger - the amygdala sounds the alarm. It's what makes your heart race when you're excited or scared.

The Hippocampus: This is like the city's grand library. It remembers the past, stores memories, and connects them to emotions. Ever smelled cookies and remembered grandma's kitchen? Or heard a song that took you back to a special moment? That's the hippocampus working its magic.

The Prefrontal Cortex: Think of this as the city's sophisticated planning committee. It weighs decisions, thinks about consequences, and tries to guide your actions sensibly. When you decide to hold your tongue instead of lashing out or take a deep breath and count to ten, that's the prefrontal cortex at play.

Survival Instincts: The Tale of Fight, Flight, or Freeze

Imagine walking through a forest and suddenly spotting a bear. Your heart races, palms sweat, and three primary choices loom large: do you stand your ground (fight), run away (flight), or become utterly still, hoping you go unnoticed (freeze)?

This isn't just about bears, though. Throughout our history, these responses have been crucial survival tools. They're the body's built-in alarm system, designed to keep us safe.

Fight: This doesn't necessarily mean throwing punches. In modern times, it might be facing a challenge head-on, like standing up against an unfair situation.

Flight: Sometimes, the best option is to remove ourselves from a harmful situation quickly. It's that gut feeling telling you to step away from a heated argument or leave a toxic environment.

Freeze: And sometimes, our bodies just... pause. It's a way of buying time, deciding the best course of action or, in some cases, hoping the danger passes us by.

By understanding these elements, the messengers, landmarks, and our innate reactions, we start to see a picture of how our internal control room operates. The world of emotions is a complex one, but at its core, it's a beautiful interplay of biology and experience. As we journey further, we'll uncover more about this intricate dance and learn how to navigate the ever-evolving landscape of our feelings.

Chapter 2: Behind the Scenes: How Our Thoughts Shape Our Emotions

The Power of Perception: Introducing the Appraisal Theory

Picture this: two friends walk through a dark, creepy forest. One thinks it's a grand adventure, while the other is utterly terrified. Same place, different reactions. Why? This brings us to the Appraisal Theory.

At its heart, the Appraisal Theory is like being a film director in the movie of your life. It's about how you "direct" or interpret a situation. The forest isn't inherently scary or adventurous. Instead, how each friend appraises or judges the forest determines their emotional response. So, if you think of challenges as opportunities, you might feel excitement instead of dread. It's all in the perspective.

When One Plus One Equals Three: The Two-Factor Theory

Ever been on a roller coaster? Heart racing, palms sweaty, adrenaline pumping? Now, was that excitement or fear? This is where the Two-Factor Theory comes into play.

This theory suggests emotions are like a two-step dance:

Physical Response: First, you experience the raw sensations, like the racing heart on that roller coaster.

Interpretation: Next, you give that feeling a name. You decide if it's thrill or terror.

So, it's not just about what you're feeling physically; it's also about how you label that feeling. The same fluttering in your stomach could be love or nervousness, depending on the situation and your interpretation.

A Peek Inside the Workshop: Cognitive Neuroscience of Emotion

Alright, it might sound a bit sci-fi, but bear with us. Imagine there's a workshop in your brain where emotions are crafted. The tools? Your thoughts and memories.

Cognitive Neuroscience of Emotion is like the study of that workshop. It seeks to understand how our brain uses past experiences, current thoughts, and expectations to mold our feelings. Remember crying during a sad movie? It's not just because of the story on screen. It's also about personal memories, experiences, and thoughts that the film brings to mind. Your brain merges the movie's narrative with your personal tales, and voila, tears flow!

In essence, our emotions aren't just spontaneous reactions. They're interwoven with our thoughts, memories, and perceptions. It's like baking a cake: the raw ingredients are our physical reactions, and the recipe is our cognitive process. Together, they create the rich, layered experience of human emotion. So, next time you're caught in a whirlwind of feelings, remember: you're not just a passive spectator. You're the director, the interpreter, and the storyteller of your emotional journey.

Chapter 3: The Melting Pot of Feelings: How Society and Culture Craft Our Emotions

Building Emotions Together: The Social Construction Theory

Imagine for a moment you're an artist. Instead of painting alone in a quiet studio, you're in a bustling plaza, surrounded by other artists and spectators, all giving input on your masterpiece. This scene captures the essence of the Social Construction Theory.

Simply put, this theory proposes that our emotions aren't just personal experiences. They're crafted in collaboration with the world around us. Just like that artwork, your feelings are influenced by friends, family, strangers, and the collective vibes of society. Ever felt the infectious energy of a cheering crowd at a concert? That's social construction in action. The group's collective enthusiasm amplifies your joy.

The Ingredients of Emotion: How Society and Culture Shape Feelings

Imagine emotions as dishes served at a global buffet. The core ingredients might be universal, but each region adds its unique spices and flavors.

Emotions don't exist in a vacuum. They're deeply intertwined with our surroundings. For instance, the pride you feel graduating from school? It's not just personal achievement; it's also shaped by societal values that champion education. The shame of making a mistake in public? That too is influenced by cultural norms around honor and dignity.

A World of Feelings: How Different Cultures Express Emotion

Travel the world, and you'll quickly realize that laughter and tears are universal. However, the reasons for them and how they're displayed can vary widely from one corner of the globe to another.

In some cultures, showing strong emotions openly, like weeping in public, might be a sign of sincerity and depth. In others, the same act might be seen as a lack of self-control. Then there are emotions that are unique to certain cultures. For instance, the concept of "Ubuntu" in African philosophy emphasizes communal values and interconnectedness. It's more than just a feeling; it's a way of life.

Think of emotions as languages. The basic grammar – joy, sorrow, anger, love – might be universal, but each culture has its dialects, idioms, and nuances.

The next time you feel a surge of emotion, pause and think: Is this just about you, or is it a symphony of influences – from friends, family, society, and even history? Understanding the social and cultural threads woven into our emotional fabric doesn't diminish our feelings. Instead, it adds depth, making the tapestry of human emotion even more intricate and beautiful.

Chapter 4: Colors of the Heart: Navigating the Wide World of Feelings

The Fundamentals: The Six Cornerstones of Emotion

Imagine a painter's palette, with six vibrant, primary colors. Just as an artist mixes these to create a masterpiece, our emotional landscape begins with six foundational feelings.

Love: It's the warm, comforting hue. The feeling when a puppy curls up beside you, or when you're embraced by a loved one.

Joy: This color dances and sparkles. It's the laughter shared with friends, the feeling of sun on your skin, or hearing your favorite song.

Anger: A fiery, intense shade. It rises when someone cuts in line, or when you see injustice.

Sadness: A deeper, melancholic tone. It's the weight in your chest when you bid goodbye, or the quiet of a rainy day.

Fear: The chilling, sharp streak. It's the jolt when the lights go out, or the heartbeat's race in a suspense movie.

Surprise: A sudden splash of unexpected color. The jump when a friend shouts "boo!" or the awe of seeing a shooting star.

Each emotion, like a color, has its place and purpose. They paint the scenes of our lives, from mundane moments to unforgettable memories.

Beyond the Basics: The Intricate Dance of Complex Emotions

While the basic emotions lay the groundwork, our emotional realm is filled with intricate shades and blends. Enter the complex emotions:

Guilt: The tug when you know you've made a mistake, a blend of regret and responsibility.

Shame: The desire to hide, to disappear. It's deeper than guilt, connected to our very sense of self.

Jealousy: That twinge when someone has what you desire. A mix of yearning, resentment, and often, self-doubt.

Pride: The swell in your chest when you or your loved ones achieve something. It's joy, mixed with a sense of accomplishment.

Just like artists combine primary colors to get intricate shades, our experiences blend basic emotions to give rise to these multifaceted feelings.

From Light to Shadow: The Emotional Spectrum

Think of emotions on a slider, moving from the brightest euphoria to the darkest despair.

Euphoria sits at the zenith, that exhilarating high, where the world feels perfect. It's the burst of elation, the feeling that you're on top of the world.

Slide towards the middle, and you find the daily ups and downs, the contentment, the mild annoyances, and fleeting joys.

Further down, we encounter Despair, the rock-bottom of emotions. It's the abyss where hope feels lost, where the world seems unbearably heavy.

But remember, the beauty of this spectrum is its fluidity. Emotions flow, change, and evolve. A moment of despair can lead to newfound understanding, and euphoria can give way to reflection.

Our emotions, in their myriad shades and intensities, create the rich tapestry of human experience. They're like music notes, creating symphonies of experiences. By understanding this vast landscape, we become better navigators of our hearts, embracing each emotion as a valuable part of our journey.

Chapter 5: The Inner Compass: Navigating Life with Emotional Intelligence

Tuning into the Heart's Frequency: What is Emotional Intelligence?

Imagine driving a car with a super-advanced GPS system. This GPS doesn't just show roads; it senses the mood in the car, predicts potential roadblocks of anger or impatience, and guides you smoothly to your destination. That's Emotional Intelligence (EI) for you, but for life.

At its essence, EI is about:

Self-awareness: Recognizing and understanding our own emotions.

Empathy: Tuning into others' feelings.

Regulation: Managing our emotions in various situations.

Motivation: Using our feelings to achieve goals.

Social skills: Interacting harmoniously with others.

Why is this important? Because life isn't just about logical choices. It's also about navigating the stormy seas of emotions, both ours and others'. Having EI is like having a compass and an anchor rolled into one.

Choices from the Heart: How Emotions Influence Decisions

Ever made a "gut decision"? Or felt "something was off" about a situation? That's your emotional compass at work.

While our brain is a decision-making powerhouse, it doesn't operate in isolation. Emotions play a starring role. They're like background music in a movie, setting the tone and influencing outcomes. For instance, if you're in a cheerful mood, you might be more likely to take risks, while anxiety can make you more cautious.

However, high EI ensures that these emotions don't lead us astray. It allows us to recognize our emotional state and factor it in, ensuring our decisions are balanced, not just impulsive reactions.

Boosting Your Emotional GPS: Ways to Enhance Emotional Intelligence

Just like any skill, EI can be honed and improved. Here are some techniques:

Reflective Journaling: Spend a few minutes daily jotting down your emotions and the reasons behind them. Over time, you'll see patterns and gain insights into your emotional self.

Active Listening: When conversing, truly tune into the other person. This will not only enhance understanding but also cultivate empathy.

Meditation and Mindfulness: By being in the moment, you become more attuned to your emotional state. It's like tuning a radio to catch the clearest frequency.

Feedback Loop: Every now and then, ask trusted friends or family about your reactions. Sometimes, an outside perspective can provide valuable insights.

Read Widely: Fiction, especially, allows you to walk in another person's shoes, fostering empathy and understanding.

Emotional Intelligence is more than just a buzzword. It's a guiding light, helping us sail smoothly even when emotional storms hit. By understanding and mastering our inner compass, we not only enhance our personal well-being but also our connections with others. After all, life's journey is not just about the destination but also about understanding and cherishing the emotions that light up the path.

Chapter 6: Steering Our Emotional Ship: Understanding and Managing Life's Tides

The Blueprint of Emotional Balance: An Introduction to Emotion Regulation Theories

Picture this: You're a sailor, and emotions are the unpredictable waters you navigate. Some days, they're calm and serene; other days, they're tempestuous and wild. Now, imagine if you had a map, a manual, or even a trusty compass that helped you through these waters. Emotion regulation theories offer us this guidance.

At their core, these theories present a simple idea: While we can't control the ocean of emotions, we can certainly choose how to sail through them. It's about understanding the waves (emotions), recognizing when a storm might be brewing, and knowing when to drop anchor or change direction.

Sailing Smoothly: Techniques to Regulate and Navigate Emotions

Ever been told to "take a deep breath" when you're upset? That's a basic emotion regulation strategy in action. Here are some of the most effective tools in our emotional toolkit:

Cognitive Reappraisal: Think of it as adjusting your emotional telescope. It involves looking at a situation from a different angle. Stuck in rain? Instead of getting frustrated, savor the beauty of raindrops or the scent of fresh earth.

Distraction: Sometimes, the best strategy is to divert your mind temporarily. Engage in a hobby, read a book, or take a walk. It's like allowing stormy waters to calm down before continuing the journey.

Expressive Suppression: Occasionally, it might be beneficial to consciously reduce our emotional reactions, especially in high-stakes situations. It's like steadying the boat when big waves come, ensuring it doesn't capsize.

Mindful Acceptance: Embracing our feelings, not fighting them. By acknowledging our emotions, we prevent them from overwhelming us.

Building an Emotional Fortress: The Power of Resilience and Well-being

Emotional resilience isn't about avoiding storms; it's about learning to sail through them. It's the strength that lets us face challenges, bounce back from setbacks, and, most importantly, learn from them.

Boosting resilience leads to a greater sense of well-being. Here are ways to fortify our emotional fortress:

Social Support: Sharing and connecting with loved ones can be an anchor during tough times. They provide comfort, perspective, and occasionally, a new direction.

Self-Care Rituals: Activities like exercise, meditation, or simply indulging in favorite hobbies can replenish our emotional energy.

Positive Thinking: This doesn't mean ignoring problems but focusing on solutions and silver linings.

Continuous Learning: Treating challenges as learning opportunities. Every storm faced and navigated teaches us valuable lessons for future voyages.

Our emotional journey is filled with ebbs and flows, highs and lows, calm seas, and stormy nights. With the right tools, understanding, and resilience, we can ensure that no matter how tumultuous the waters, we remain the skilled sailors of our emotional ship, ready for whatever adventures life brings our way.

Chapter 7: The Domino Effect: Emotions in Our Social Dance

The Ripple Effect: How Emotions Influence Our Social Ties

Picture a quiet pond. Toss a pebble into it. See the ripples it creates? That's what emotions do in our social world. Every smile, frown, tear, or laugh has an impact – sometimes obvious, sometimes subtle.

For instance, have you ever walked into a room and felt the tension without anyone saying a word? Or felt inexplicably happy around someone who's joyful? Emotions, it seems, have a language of their own. They can bridge gaps, build bonds, or occasionally, build walls.

Catching Feelings: Understanding Emotional Contagion and Empathy

Emotions are, surprisingly, quite contagious! Just like a yawn can travel through a room, so can feelings.

Emotional Contagion: Ever found yourself feeling down after speaking to a gloomy friend? Or suddenly energetic around an enthusiastic colleague? Emotions, both positive and negative, can 'rub off' on us. It's an unconscious process, like tuning our radio to someone else's frequency.

Empathy: If emotional contagion is catching someone's tune, empathy is understanding the lyrics. It's feeling someone's joy or pain and comprehending their perspective. It's a deeper connection, allowing us to not just sense but share emotions.

Both these phenomena underline a fundamental truth: We're wired to connect. Our emotions are tools that help, hinder, or enhance these connections.

Navigating Emotional Storms: Emotions in Conflict and Resolution

Conflicts are an inevitable part of our social dance. Emotions play both the role of the instigator and the peacemaker.

Emotions as Sparks: A misinterpreted tone, envy, pride, or anger can lead to disagreements. Emotions can amplify misunderstandings, turning them into conflicts.

Emotions as Bridges: On the flip side, emotions can also heal. Genuine remorse, understanding, or compassion can mend rifts. A heartfelt apology or a sincere talk can rebuild bridges that anger might have burnt.

Understanding the role of emotions in conflicts can be the key to resolving them. It's about recognizing when emotions are escalating a situation and using them effectively to de-escalate. For instance, using empathy to see the other person's point of view or harnessing calm to approach a tense situation.

As social beings, our emotional world is intricately tied to those around us. Like dominoes, a shift in one piece (or person) can set off a cascade. By understanding the power and pull of emotions in our interpersonal interactions, we can become better dance partners in the intricate ballet of social life, syncing our steps and ensuring the dance floor remains harmonious.

Chapter 8: Heartstrings: The Emotional Symphony of Relationships

The Ties that Bind: Attachment Theory and Love

Ever wondered why we're drawn to certain people or why some relationships leave deeper imprints than others? Think of it like gravity; an invisible force pulling two celestial bodies together.

In the world of relationships, this gravitational pull is guided by the Attachment Theory. In simple terms, it's about how our early relationships (like the bond with our parents) influence our future ones.

Imagine our hearts have a unique type of 'memory.' This memory recalls how we were loved, cared for, or let down as kids. As we grow, these memories shape our 'love style'. Some of us become fiercely independent, others might always seek closeness, and a few might often feel mixed—yearning for intimacy yet fearing it.

Understanding our attachment style can be like finding a map of our emotional terrain, helping us navigate the peaks and valleys of love more smoothly.

The Spark and the Flame: Emotions and Sexual Attraction

While love is a profound emotional connection, sexual attraction is that initial electric spark. It's what often lights the fire, making our cheeks flush, heart race, or gives us those famous "butterflies."

But, what's behind this spark? Emotions play a key role, adding depth and color to attraction. It's like the difference between a blank canvas and a passionate painting. Emotions infuse this canvas with excitement, nervousness, desire, or even vulnerability.

Recognizing the interplay of emotions and attraction is crucial. It ensures we understand the difference between a fleeting flame and a lasting ember.

Mending the Broken Strings: Coping with Loss and Heartbreak

The journey of love isn't always smooth. Sometimes, it takes us through the dark tunnels of loss and heartbreak. Whether it's a relationship ending, unrequited love, or the passing of a loved one, the emotional toll can be immense.

But why does it hurt so much? Because emotions, especially love, create deep-rooted connections. Breaking them feels like tearing a part of ourselves away.

Navigating this pain requires:

Acknowledgment: Accepting our feelings, not suppressing them.

Support: Leaning on loved ones or professionals for guidance.

Self-Care: Healing isn't linear. It's crucial to be gentle with ourselves, taking time to grieve, recover, and eventually, rebuild.

Finding Closure: Sometimes, understanding why something ended can help in moving forward.

Love, with its myriad shades, paints our life's canvas like no other emotion. Whether it's the rosy hues of romance, the passionate reds of attraction, or the blues of heartbreak, understanding these emotions can make our relationship journey more enriching and, ultimately, more fulfilling. Because at the end of the day, it's these heartstrings that play the most beautiful symphonies of our lives.

Chapter 9: Digital Heartbeats: Navigating Emotions in the Age of Screens

Pixelated Feelings: How Technology Influences Emotion Perception and Expression

Imagine the days when a heartfelt letter was the primary mode of distant communication. The written word was potent, yes, but limited. Now, flash forward to today, where emojis, GIFs, and video chats reign supreme.

Technology, especially the digital kind, has redefined the way we "see" and "show" emotions. A crying emoji can represent sadness, joy, or even frustration. But sometimes, nuances get lost. The subtlety of a soft smile or the glint in a person's eye during a joke can't always be captured in pixels.

While digital tools allow us to express emotions in innovative ways, they also challenge us. It's easy to misinterpret a message's tone or to feel the pressure to curate our emotions to fit a screen-friendly version.

The Social Media Rollercoaster: From Likes to Loathes

Social media platforms, where emotions are often at the forefront, can feel like a rollercoaster. One minute, you're on top of the world with likes and positive comments, and the next, you might be spiraling from a negative remark or comparison.

Platforms like Instagram, Twitter, and Facebook amplify our emotions:

Joy and Validation: That rush when your post is appreciated.

Loneliness and Envy: Scrolling through perfect-looking lives, feeling yours isn't up to par.

Anger and Polarization: Getting involved in heated online debates.

Recognizing these emotional highs and lows can help us use social media more mindfully, understanding when it's time to unplug or filter our feeds.

Stepping into Another World: Virtual Reality and Emotions

Have you ever wished to escape reality? With the advent of Virtual Reality (VR), this is becoming more feasible. VR immerses us in digital realms, allowing us to experience emotions in novel ways.

Imagine facing your fears in a controlled environment, like standing atop a virtual skyscraper if you're scared of heights. Or, feeling the euphoria of flying through magical lands.

But, as with every tool, balance is key. While VR can be a portal to wonderful experiences, it's essential to ensure we don't lose touch with the real world's emotional richness.

The Digital Age, with its array of gadgets and platforms, offers a mixed bag of emotional experiences. As we continue to merge our lives with technology, understanding its impact on our feelings becomes essential. After all, while screens might change, the human heart – with its capacity for myriad emotions – remains constant. In this age, it's about finding the perfect balance between digital heart-beats and the real, unfiltered pulse of life.

Chapter 10: Feeling Forward: Emotion, the Ultimate Odyssey

Unraveling the Tapestry: Emotions and the Human Condition

At the very core of our existence, amidst all our achievements, ambitions, and dreams, lie our emotions. They've been with us from our very first cry as infants to our most profound moments as adults. It's these emotions that have colored our memories, turning some black and white moments into vibrant technicolor.

But why do we feel? What purpose do these sensations serve? Emotions are not just reactions; they're a language. They communicate our needs, desires, and fears. They're the compass that has guided humanity through millennia, from survival in the wild to intricate social networks. In essence, our emotions are the heartbeat of the human condition.

Beyond Today: The Exciting Horizon of Emotion Research

While we've come a long way in understanding our emotional world, there's still much terrain left unexplored. The future of emotion research is brimming with potential:

Neuroscience & Beyond: With advancements in brain imaging, we're getting closer to pinpointing how emotions manifest in our minds.

AI and Emotions: As artificial intelligence becomes an integral part of our lives, how will machines recognize or even 'feel' emotions?

Interstellar Emotions: As we dream of interplanetary travels, how will the vastness of space impact our emotional landscape?

These questions and more pave the way for a future where understanding emotions might be the key to unlocking newer realms of human potential.

Echoes of the Heart: The Power and Promise of Emotions

If there's one thing to take away from our journey into the world of emotions, it's this: emotions are potent. They've started revolutions, inspired masterpieces, and forged connections that time or distance couldn't break.

Our capacity to feel deeply is both our greatest strength and vulnerability. Emotions drive us, motivate us, and occasionally, challenge us. They are the silent threads weaving the tapestry of our lives.

As we stand on the brink of a future where the lines between man, machine, and cosmos blur, it's our emotions that will guide us, anchor us, and remind us of our shared humanity.

In concluding this odyssey, always remember: To feel is to be human. Embrace it, understand it, and most importantly, cherish it. For in the vast universe of experiences, it's our emotions that truly make us alive.

About Freudian Trips

Welcome to Freudian Trips, your dedicated platform for diving deep into the world of psychology. We are more than just a YouTube channel or a book publisher. We are a beacon of enlightenment, making complex psychological concepts accessible and engaging for all.

Our YouTube channel is a rich repository of psychology made simple. We take the profound and often complex ideas from the world of psychology and break them down into digestible, easy-to-understand content. From the foundational theories of Freud to the cognitive insights of Piaget, we cover a broad spectrum of psychological schools and thoughts, making psychology accessible to everyone, regardless of their background or prior knowledge.

As a book publisher, we take the same approach, transforming intricate psychological theories into comprehensible narratives. Our books are not just collections of words, but vessels of wisdom that make psychology approachable and relatable. We believe that psychology should not be confined to academic circles, but should be available to all who seek to understand the human mind and behavior.

At Freudian Trips, we believe in the power of curiosity and the pursuit of knowledge. We are here to stoke the fires of your curiosity, to guide you on your intellectual journey, and to help you navigate the fascinating world of psychology.

If you are someone who is not afraid to question, to explore, and to learn, then you are in the right place. Join us on this journey of exploration, as we make psychology easy to understand, one concept at a time.

Be sure to visit our Youtube channel at: www.freudiantrips.com/youtube

You can also visit us on the web at www.freudiantrips.com

Welcome to The Freudian Trip community. Stay curious. Stay enlightened.

www.ingramcontent.com/pod-product-compliance
Lightning Source LLC
Chambersburg PA
CBHW071613270726
48661CB00019B/3429